The Duck and the Frog

Alison Frontin

Illustrations by Windel Eborlas

To order additional copies of this book, contact:
Xlibris
1-888-795-4274
www.Xlibris.com
Orders@Xlibris.com

The Duck and the Frog

This is book dedicated to Kayla Headley.

As a man and his friend were fishing,
A duck came along in the muddy pond.
Looking for her mother,
But she cannot be found

Who is on my back?
Was her quacking sound.

It's me. I'm Mr. Frog.
I am lost, and it's a big cost,
But you I can trust
To take me over this course.

My color is green.
I make a lovely scene.
I can hop and not talk.

I came for a walk and,
I got lost,
I saw you and you made no fuss.
Can you take me over this course?

Sometimes I rock,
But I don't wear a frock.
Neither does my mouth lock.

Look for me if you can.
Can you take me to the sand?
There we can be perfect fans.

I swim on my belly.
Sometimes I reach close to the jetty.

People watch me and throw
Me some pennies.
I can share with you, but
Don't look for many.

We can sit and talk
And watch people walk
And have fun in the hot sun.

I can see a crown on your head
Made out of corn.
I am unhappy I am in the pond.

I have two webbed feet
That keep me on the beat
And a long beak
I can use to reach things to eat

Mr. Frog, there is a fair over there,
And I can see a log, my dear.
We can sit on our rear.
We are a picturesque pair.

Ribbit, ribbit, said Mr. Frog.
I can see your color is yellow.
It reminds me of a fellow
Whose name was Mr. Sello.

I see your feathers.
It's very good for the rainy weather,
And at no time you look withered.

My name is Raad.
I never get mad
Even though people try
To give me massive jabs.

My color is green,
Sometimes brown.
I never got worn or torn.
I just love being on the ground.

My tongue is very long.
I can't sing a song
But can catch many flies.
They never thought they would die.

I have two feet I use to hop.
They carry me along, I never drop.
I have two eyes some people try to salt at times.

My skin is thick, I hardly get sick.
I don't visit the doctor a bit.
Here I am, very healthy and can sit.

There is a church
Let's go and boast,
We love the Lord most

Let's pray for peace,
War to cease,
And we will be like,
Peas in the pod.

Now we can go our different ways
And be so amazed
And hope we meet at a later day.

Printed in the United States
By Bookmasters